ALABASTER

ALABASTER

Printed in Canada

Contact
hello@alabasterco.com
www.alabasterco.com

Alabaster Co. The Bible Beautiful.
Visual imagery & thoughtful design integrated within the Bible.
Cultivating conversation between art, beauty, & faith.

Founded in 2016.

NLT.

ARTIST INTRODUCTION

———

Written in beautiful, poetic language, Song of Songs celebrates a universal desire of humanity—love. It is a window into the type of love God intended for all of us since the Garden of Eden. It is an invitation to enjoy—with wisdom, obedience, and prudence—the gifts of passion, love, and sexual desire.

We explore these themes through several motifs. While some of the language in Song of Songs translates well to our contemporary perceptions, much of it is written in a more ancient, allegorical context and understanding. We aid these poems with modern textural and abstracted elements, to speak to and heighten our sensibilities of love. We frequently depict subjects of two, to mirror the relationship between the two lovers in the book. And we create images with a tasteful aesthetic— sought to depict the biblical ideas of passion and desire within the book.

Like all good poetry, Song of Songs is meant to invite us on a journey of contemplation and exploration—to be enjoyed, chewed on, and imagined about. And ultimately, as it has been interpreted by many Christians throughout history, the passion demonstrated by the two lovers can be representative of God's endless love for all of humanity. May we seek and enjoy love. Amen.

THE

SONG OF SONGS

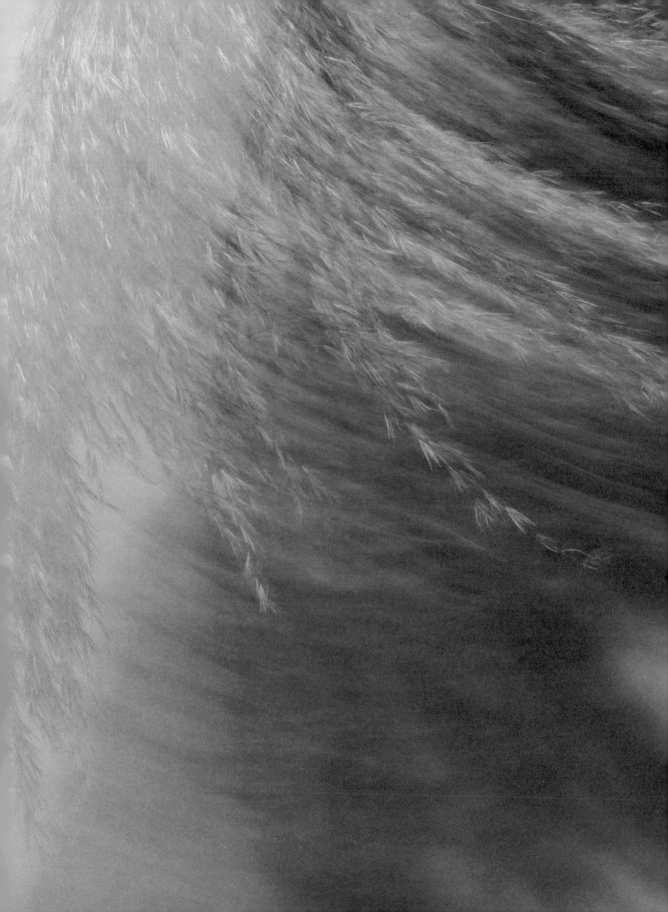

1

¹ This is Solomon's song of songs, more wonderful than any other.

YOUNG WOMAN

² Kiss me and kiss me again,
  for your love is sweeter than wine.
³ How pleasing is your fragrance; your name is like
  the spreading fragrance of scented oils.
  No wonder all the young women love you!
⁴ Take me with you; come, let's run!
  The king has brought me into his bedroom.

YOUNG WOMEN OF JERUSALEM

How happy we are for you, O king.
We praise your love even more than wine.

YOUNG WOMAN

How right they are to adore you.

5 I am dark but beautiful,
O women of Jerusalem—
dark as the tents of Kedar,
dark as the curtains of Solomon's tents.

6 Don't stare at me because I am dark—
the sun has darkened my skin.
My brothers were angry with me;
they forced me to care for their vineyards,
so I couldn't care for myself—my own vineyard.

7 Tell me, my love, where are you leading
your flock today?
Where will you rest your sheep at noon?
For why should I wander like a prostitute
among your friends and their flocks?

YOUNG MAN

8 If you don't know, O most beautiful woman,
follow the trail of my flock,
and graze your young goats by the shepherds' tents.

9 You are as exciting, my darling,
as a mare among Pharaoh's stallions.

10 How lovely are your cheeks;
your earrings set them afire!
How lovely is your neck,
enhanced by a string of jewels.

11 We will make for you earrings of gold
and beads of silver.

YOUNG WOMAN

12 The king is lying on his couch,
enchanted by the fragrance of my perfume.

13 My lover is like a sachet of myrrh
lying between my breasts.

14 He is like a bouquet of sweet henna blossoms
from the vineyards of En-gedi.

YOUNG MAN

[15] How beautiful you are, my darling,
how beautiful!
Your eyes are like doves.

YOUNG WOMAN

16 You are so handsome, my love,
pleasing beyond words!
The soft grass is our bed;

17 fragrant cedar branches are the beams of our house,
and pleasant smelling firs are the rafters.

2

YOUNG WOMAN

[1] I am the spring crocus blooming on the Sharon Plain,
the lily of the valley.

YOUNG MAN

[2] Like a lily among thistles
is my darling among young women.

YOUNG WOMAN

[3] Like the finest apple tree in the orchard
is my lover among other young men.
I sit in his delightful shade
and taste his delicious fruit.

⁴ He escorts me to the banquet hall;
it's obvious how much he loves me.

⁵ Strengthen me with raisin cakes,
refresh me with apples,
for I am weak with love.

⁶ His left arm is under my head,
and his right arm embraces me.

⁷ Promise me, O women of Jerusalem,
by the gazelles and wild deer,
not to awaken love until the time is right.

⁸ Ah, I hear my lover coming!
He is leaping over the mountains,
bounding over the hills.

⁹ My lover is like a swift gazelle
or a young stag.

Look, there he is behind the wall,
looking through the window,
peering into the room.

¹⁰ My lover said to me,
"Rise up, my darling!
Come away with me, my fair one!

¹¹ Look, the winter is past,
and the rains are over and gone.

¹² The flowers are springing up,
the season of singing birds has come,
and the cooing of turtledoves fills the air.

¹³ The fig trees are forming young fruit,
and the fragrant grapevines are blossoming.
Rise up, my darling!
Come away with me, my fair one!"

YOUNG MAN

14 My dove is hiding behind the rocks,
   behind an outcrop on the cliff.
   Let me see your face;
   let me hear your voice.
   For your voice is pleasant,
   and your face is lovely.

YOUNG WOMEN OF JERUSALEM

15 Catch all the foxes,
   those little foxes,
   before they ruin the vineyard of love,
   for the grapevines are blossoming!

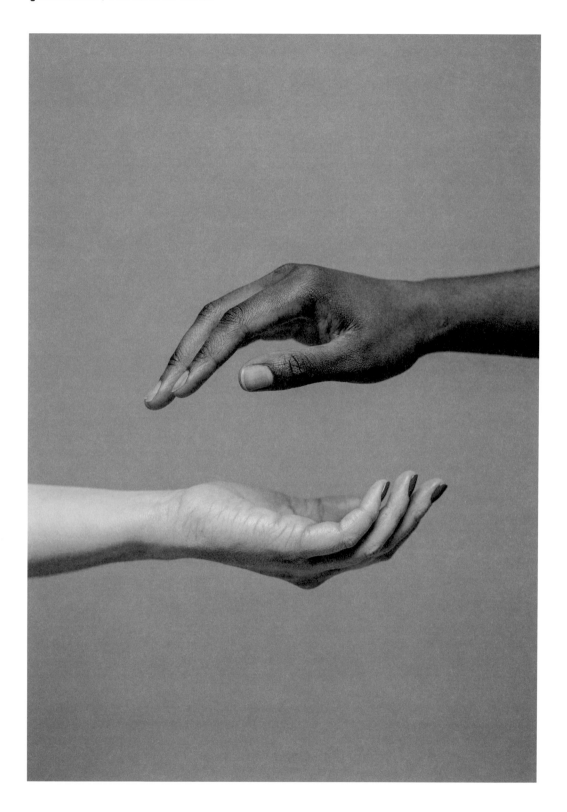

YOUNG WOMAN

[16] My lover is mine, and I am his.
He browses among the lilies.

[17] Before the dawn breezes blow
and the night shadows flee,
return to me, my love, like a gazelle
or a young stag on the rugged mountains.

3

YOUNG WOMAN

1 One night as I lay in bed, I yearned for my lover.
I yearned for him, but he did not come.

2 So I said to myself, "I will get up and roam the city,
searching in all its streets and squares.
I will search for the one I love."
So I searched everywhere but did not find him.

3 The watchmen stopped me as they made their rounds,
and I asked, "Have you seen the one I love?"

4 Then scarcely had I left them
when I found my love!
I caught and held him tightly,
then I brought him to my mother's house,
into my mother's bed, where I had been conceived.

5 Promise me, O women of Jerusalem,
by the gazelles and wild deer,
not to awaken love until the time is right.

YOUNG WOMEN OF JERUSALEM

6 Who is this sweeping in from the wilderness
like a cloud of smoke?
Who is it, fragrant with myrrh and frankincense
and every kind of spice?

7   Look, it is Solomon's carriage,
    surrounded by sixty heroic men,
    the best of Israel's soldiers.
8   They are all skilled swordsmen,
    experienced warriors.
    Each wears a sword on his thigh,
    ready to defend the king against an attack in the night.
9   King Solomon's carriage is built
    of wood imported from Lebanon.
10 Its posts are silver,
    its canopy gold;
    its cushions are purple.
    It was decorated with love
    by the young women of Jerusalem.

YOUNG WOMAN

11 Come out to see King Solomon,
    young women of Jerusalem.
    He wears the crown his mother
    gave him on his wedding day,
    his most joyous day.

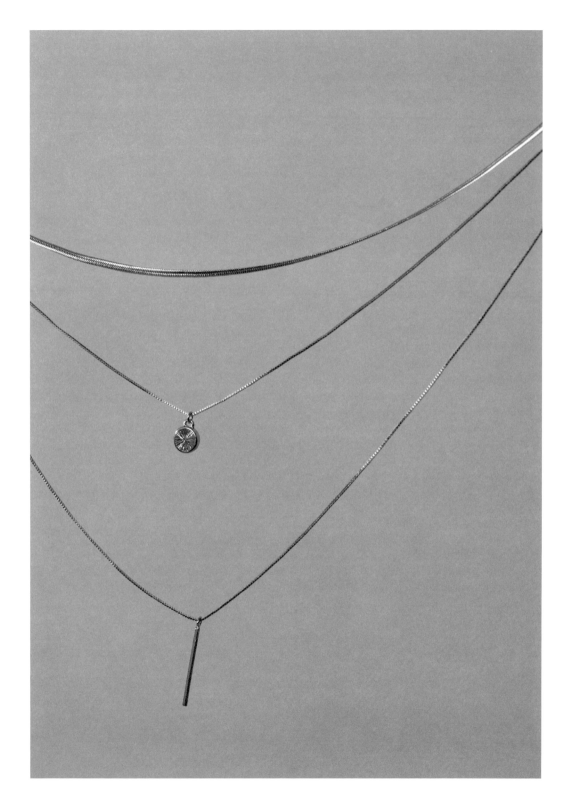

4

YOUNG MAN

1 You are beautiful, my darling,
beautiful beyond words.
Your eyes are like doves
behind your veil.
Your hair falls in waves,
like a flock of goats winding down the slopes of Gilead.

2 Your teeth are as white as sheep,
recently shorn and freshly washed.
Your smile is flawless,
each tooth matched with its twin.

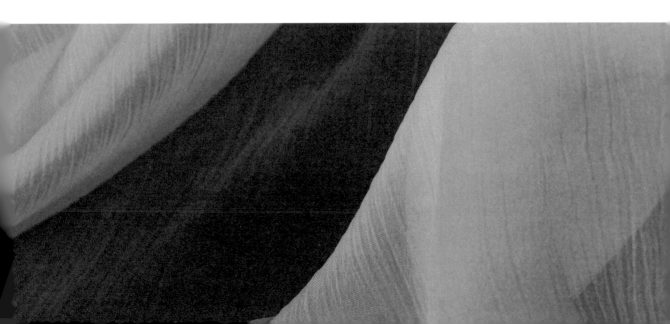

[3] Your lips are like scarlet ribbon;
your mouth is inviting.
Your cheeks are like rosy pomegranates
behind your veil.

[4] Your neck is as beautiful as the tower of David,
jeweled with the shields of a thousand heroes.

[5] Your breasts are like two fawns,
twin fawns of a gazelle grazing among the lilies.

[6] Before the dawn breezes blow
and the night shadows flee,
I will hurry to the mountain of myrrh
and to the hill of frankincense.

[7] You are altogether beautiful, my darling,
beautiful in every way.

[8] Come with me from Lebanon, my bride,
come with me from Lebanon.
Come down from Mount Amana,
from the peaks of Senir and Hermon,
where the lions have their dens
and leopards live among the hills.

[9] You have captured my heart,
my treasure, my bride.
You hold it hostage with one glance of your eyes,
with a single jewel of your necklace.

[10] Your love delights me,
my treasure, my bride.
Your love is better than wine,
your perfume more fragrant than spices.

[11] Your lips are as sweet as nectar, my bride.
Honey and milk are under your tongue.
Your clothes are scented
like the cedars of Lebanon.

¹² You are my private garden, my treasure, my bride,
a secluded spring, a hidden fountain.
¹³ Your thighs shelter a paradise of pomegranates
with rare spices—
henna with nard,
¹⁴ nard and saffron,
fragrant calamus and cinnamon,
with all the trees of frankincense, myrrh, and aloes,
and every other lovely spice.
¹⁵ You are a garden fountain,
a well of fresh water
streaming down from Lebanon's mountains.

YOUNG WOMAN

16 Awake, north wind!
Rise up, south wind!
Blow on my garden
and spread its fragrance all around.
Come into your garden, my love;
taste its finest fruits.

5

YOUNG MAN

¹ I have entered my garden, my treasure, my bride!
I gather myrrh with my spices
and eat honeycomb with my honey.
I drink wine with my milk.

YOUNG WOMEN OF JERUSALEM

Oh, lover and beloved, eat and drink!
Yes, drink deeply of your love!

YOUNG WOMAN

² I slept, but my heart was awake,
when I heard my lover knocking and calling:
"Open to me, my treasure, my darling,
my dove, my perfect one.
My head is drenched with dew,
my hair with the dampness of the night."

³ But I responded,
   "I have taken off my robe.
   Should I get dressed again?
   I have washed my feet.
   Should I get them soiled?"
⁴ My lover tried to unlatch the door,
   and my heart thrilled within me.
⁵ I jumped up to open the door for my love,
   and my hands dripped with perfume.
   My fingers dripped with lovely myrrh
   as I pulled back the bolt.
⁶ I opened to my lover,
   but he was gone!
   My heart sank.
   I searched for him
   but could not find him anywhere.
   I called to him,
   but there was no reply.

[7] The night watchmen found me
as they made their rounds.
They beat and bruised me
and stripped off my veil,
those watchmen on the walls.

[8] Make this promise, O women of Jerusalem—
If you find my lover,
tell him I am weak with love.

YOUNG WOMEN OF JERUSALEM

[9] Why is your lover better than all others,
O woman of rare beauty?
What makes your lover so special
that we must promise this?

YOUNG WOMAN

10 My lover is dark and dazzling,
better than ten thousand others!

11 His head is finest gold,
his wavy hair is black as a raven.

12 His eyes sparkle like doves
beside springs of water;
they are set like jewels
washed in milk.

13 His cheeks are like gardens of spices
giving off fragrance.
His lips are like lilies,
perfumed with myrrh.

14 His arms are like rounded bars of gold,
set with beryl.
His body is like bright ivory,
glowing with lapis lazuli.

15 His legs are like marble pillars

set in sockets of finest gold.
His posture is stately,
like the noble cedars of Lebanon.

16 His mouth is sweetness itself;
he is desirable in every way.
Such, O women of Jerusalem,
is my lover, my friend.

6

YOUNG WOMEN OF JERUSALEM

[1] Where has your lover gone,
O woman of rare beauty?
Which way did he turn
so we can help you find him?

YOUNG WOMAN

2 My lover has gone down to his garden,
   to his spice beds,
   to browse in the gardens
   and gather the lilies.

3 I am my lover's, and my lover is mine.
   He browses among the lilies.

YOUNG MAN

4   You are beautiful, my darling,
    like the lovely city of Tirzah.
    Yes, as beautiful as Jerusalem,
    as majestic as an army with billowing banners.

⁵ Turn your eyes away,
for they overpower me.
Your hair falls in waves,
like a flock of goats winding down the slopes of Gilead.
⁶ Your teeth are as white as sheep

that are freshly washed.
Your smile is flawless,
each tooth matched with its twin.
⁷ Your cheeks are like rosy pomegranates
behind your veil.

8 Even among sixty queens
and eighty concubines
and countless young women,
9 I would still choose my dove, my perfect one—
the favorite of her mother,
dearly loved by the one who bore her.
The young women see her and praise her;
even queens and royal concubines sing her praises:
10 "Who is this, arising like the dawn,
as fair as the moon,
as bright as the sun,
as majestic as an army with billowing banners?"

YOUNG WOMAN

11 I went down to the grove of walnut trees
and out to the valley to see the new spring growth,
to see whether the grapevines had budded
or the pomegranates were in bloom.
12 Before I realized it,
my strong desires had taken me to the chariot of
a noble man.

YOUNG WOMEN OF JERUSALEM

13 Return, return to us, O maid of Shulam.
Come back, come back, that we may see you again.

YOUNG MAN

Why do you stare at this young woman
of Shulam, as she moves so gracefully between two
lines of dancers?

7

¹ How beautiful are your sandaled feet,
O queenly maiden.
Your rounded thighs are like jewels,
the work of a skilled craftsman.
² Your navel is perfectly formed
like a goblet filled with mixed wine.
Between your thighs lies a mound of wheat
bordered with lilies.
³ Your breasts are like two fawns,
twin fawns of a gazelle.
⁴ Your neck is as beautiful as an ivory tower.
Your eyes are like the sparkling pools in Heshbon
by the gate of Bath-rabbim.
Your nose is as fine as the tower of Lebanon
overlooking Damascus.
⁵ Your head is as majestic as Mount Carmel,
and the sheen of your hair radiates royalty.
The king is held captive by its tresses.

6 Oh, how beautiful you are!
How pleasing, my love, how full of delights!

7 You are slender like a palm tree,
and your breasts are like its clusters of fruit.

8 I said, "I will climb the palm tree
and take hold of its fruit."

May your breasts be like grape clusters,

and the fragrance of your breath like apples.

⁹ May your kisses be as exciting as the best wine—

YOUNG WOMAN

Yes, wine that goes down smoothly for my lover,

flowing gently over lips and teeth.

¹⁰ I am my lover's,

and he claims me as his own.

¹¹ Come, my love, let us go out to the fields

and spend the night among the wildflowers.

¹² Let us get up early and go to the vineyards

to see if the grapevines have budded,

if the blossoms have opened,

and if the pomegranates have bloomed.

There I will give you my love.

¹³ There the mandrakes give off their fragrance,
and the finest fruits are at our door,
new delights as well as old,
which I have saved for you, my lover.

8

YOUNG WOMAN

¹ Oh, I wish you were my brother,
   who nursed at my mother's breasts.
   Then I could kiss you no matter who was watching,
   and no one would criticize me.
² I would bring you to my childhood home,
   and there you would teach me.
   I would give you spiced wine to drink,
   my sweet pomegranate wine.
³ Your left arm would be under my head,
   and your right arm would embrace me.
⁴ Promise me, O women of Jerusalem,
   not to awaken love until the time is right.

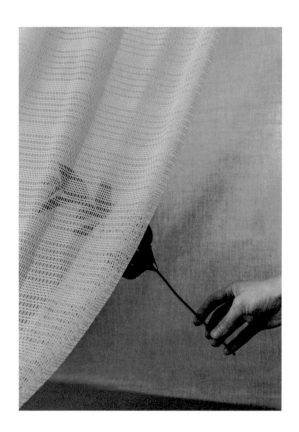

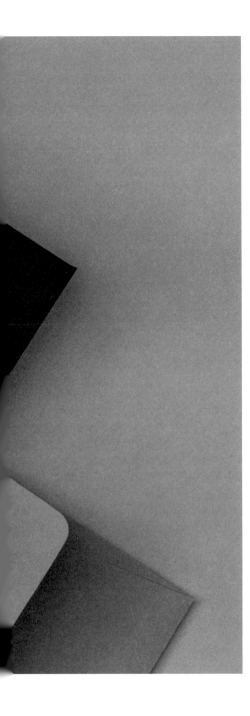

YOUNG WOMEN OF JERUSALEM

⁵ Who is this sweeping in from the desert,
leaning on her lover?

YOUNG WOMAN

I aroused you under the apple tree,
where your mother gave you birth,
where in great pain she delivered you.
⁶ Place me like a seal over your heart,
like a seal on your arm.
For love is as strong as death,
its jealousy as enduring as the grave.
Love flashes like fire,
the brightest kind of flame.
⁷ Many waters cannot quench love,
nor can rivers drown it.
If a man tried to buy love
with all his wealth,
his offer would be utterly scorned.

THE YOUNG WOMAN'S BROTHERS

8 We have a little sister
too young to have breasts.
What will we do for our sister
if someone asks to marry her?

9 If she is a virgin, like a wall,
we will protect her with a silver tower.
But if she is promiscuous, like a swinging door,
we will block her door with a cedar bar.

YOUNG WOMAN

10 I was a virgin, like a wall;
now my breasts are like towers.
When my lover looks at me,
he is delighted with what he sees.

11 Solomon has a vineyard at Baal-hamon,
which he leases out to tenant farmers.
Each of them pays a thousand pieces of silver
for harvesting its fruit.

12 But my vineyard is mine to give,
and Solomon need not pay a thousand pieces of silver.
But I will give two hundred pieces
to those who care for its vines.

YOUNG MAN

[13] O my darling, lingering in the gardens,
your companions are fortunate to hear your voice.
Let me hear it, too!

YOUNG WOMAN

[14] Come away, my love! Be like a gazelle
or a young stag on the mountains of spices.

ALABASTER

TYLER ZAK
Product Manager, Art Director

MATTHEW RAVENELLE
Layout Designer

SAMUEL HAN
Cover Image
Studio Photographer & Editor

MARK YEONGJUN SEO
Studio Stylist

ALEXIS SOOMIN LEE
Studio Assistant

BRYAN YE-CHUNG
Co-Founder, Creative Director

BRIAN CHUNG
Co-Founder, Managing Director

WILLA JIN
Operations Director

EMALY HUNTER
Customer Experience Specialist

DARIN MCKENNA
Content Editor

JOSEPHINE LAW
Original Designer

ALABASTER

PHOTOGRAPHERS

Andriana Kovalchuk   Jonathan Knepper
Bryan Ye-Chung   Lois Lee
Carmen Leung   Makito Umekita
Chester Nathanael   Mike Sunu
Echo Yun Chen   Samuel Han
Haven Kim   Sophia Hsin
Ian Teraoka   Tyler Zak
Joel Rojas

MODELS   ## PAINTINGS

Alexis Soomin Lee   Bryan Ye-Chung
Mark Yeongjun Seo

CONTINUE THE CONVERSATION

www.alabasterco.com